Grammie
Rules

49 Reasons to Spend Time with your Grandkids

by Karl
(grandpa)

ISBN: 1453634991
ISBN-13: 9781453634998

TABLE OF CONTENTS

✻ ✻ ✻

Reason #1   THE FIRST ENCOUNTER 1
Reason #2   THE BIG GUY 3
Reason #3   MOMMY WASN'T UPSET 4
Reason #4   GRAMMIE, WATCH ME SHOVEL 6
Reason #5   MADE PERFECT SENSE 7
Reason #6   WINGS OF SONG 8
Reason #7   IT'S ALL ABOUT ME 10
Reason #8   WACKENMOCKENSNOCKER 11
Reason #9   ZINGERS 12
Reason # 10   THE ONE-ARMED MAN 13
Reason # 11   YOU WORRY TOO MUCH 15
Reason # 12   NASCAR AND COUNTING 16
Reason # 13   MOVE OVER PHIL MICKELSON 17
Reason # 14   KARL, YOU'RE... 18
Reason # 15   WHY DO YOU TALK LIKE THAT? 19
Reason # 16   TV AND KARL 20
Reason # 17   FIRST ROUND OF GOLF-Learn the Rules, Karl 21
Reason # 18   FIRST ROUND OF GOLF-PART II 22
Reason # 19   OLD PEOPLE DIE 24
Reason # 20   T-BALL 25
Reason # 21   I'LL TAKE THESE, KARL, OK? 27
Reason # 22   THE GIRL IN WHITE 28
Reason # 23   I STARTED SCHOOL YESTERDAY 29
Reason # 24   THAT FIRST PICK UP 30
Reason # 25   PRINCESS LEI-A 32
Reason # 26   WHAT MOMMY TEACHES 33
Reason # 27   MORE ZINGERS 34
Reason # 28   WHAT'S A DRILL? 36
Reason # 29   I DON'T KNOW HER NAME 37
Reason # 30   SEPTEMBER 1, 2009 38

Reason # 31 MAKE THAT NOISE AGAIN 39
Reason # 32 NO HOME DEPOTS 40
Reason # 33 MOMMY SHARES A GRANDKID STORY.............. 41
Reason # 34 ANOTHER MOMMY STORY 43
Reason # 35 AGONY OF VICTORY 44
Reason # 36 GRAMMIE'S RULES 46
Reason # 37 CATTAILS.. 47
Reason # 38 GOING GREEN 49
Reason # 39 ALIENS, REALLY.. 50
Reason # 40 MOMMY, BIGGEST FISH EVER 51
Reason # 41 MORE GRANDKID STORIES............................. 52
Reason # 42 ONE FOR THE MUSEUM.................................. 54
Reason # 43 CHANGE YOUR SHIRT, MURRAY 56
Reason # 44 ZINGERS, ONE MORE TIME 58
Reason # 45 Wii GAME AND KARL...................................... 60
Reason # 46 IT'S NOT SCARY.. 61
Reason # 47 I LOST MY TOOTH.. 63
Reason # 48 I'M ALMOST SIX NOW 65
Reason # 49 THERE IS NO END...   67

———

FOREWARD

✿ ✿ ✿

These are stories about my grandson Aidan.

Aidan is not a unique grandchild. But he is special to his grandparents, and all grandparents will agree that experiences with grandchildren are one of the primary benefits of the later years.

Sharing stories about your grandkids? Well, that's almost as much fun as the experiences themselves.

These stories about Aidan are written as he approaches his sixth birthday. I wrote them because they make me smile, and someday, Aidan will remember and smile, too.

More importantly, these stories remind me of how lucky I am to have had these moments to share... and that I'm glad I've made the time to spend with him.

There are millions of grandparents out there with a story or two to share. I invite you to send me your favorite story (or two). You'll have fun reliving the event, and I guarantee others will enjoy reading your story as much as you did the actual experience.

I'm supposed to thank Rachel (a wonderful editor), Mommy, Daddy, Grammie, and two friends who read the articles for their helpful comments. But I don't have time. Aidan just arrived and said "Karl, let's play ball. You know you're my best friend."

So enjoy my Aidan stories…and then share your own.

Email your stories to *Grammierules@gmail.com*. I will select stories and compile them in a Second Edition of "Reasons To Spend Time With Your Grandkids." It will be a fun read for all ages.

Karl

REASON #1 THE FIRST ENCOUNTER

✿ ✿ ✿

Karl's first time holding "The Big Guy"

Of the many memories a hospital evokes, one of the most pleasant is hearing the cries of a newborn in the birthing center.

Aidan Michael arrived at 4:15 p.m. and weighed in at 7 pounds, 14 ounces, with 10 fingers and 10 toes, and working vocal cords. Mother was doing fine, and within hours, between the floral arrangements and relatives from three generations, it was standing room only.

Like all newborns, Aidan was admired and proclaimed "cutest" and "most darling." Photos were mandatory as he was passed from mother to grandmothers to great-grandmothers, to uncles, aunts, friends, and on to other remaining relatives. Except me.

I refused my turn to hold the Big Guy (a moniker I would later give Aidan). Among the hundreds of human fears and phobias, mine is the fear of holding (and dropping) a newborn. I really have no basis or recalled experience to justify this fear.

But the fear is real and for the first 90 days I carefully avoided picking up or holding Aidan. This behavior did not go unnoticed by Aidan's parents and his Grammie. To people who do not experience your personal fear, that fear is considered irrational and nonsense.

Finally, on the occasion of Aidan's three-month celebration (monthly events at Grammie's house until age one), I was forced to confront my fear.

Aidan's father was holding the Big Guy during a casual conversation when suddenly he said forcefully "Here, you take him," and dangled Aidan in front of me. The message was clear – either you take him or Aidan will experience his first five-foot fall.

Reflex kicked in and I found myself clutching the now 10 pound Aidan. I probably squeezed him beyond the medical limits, but Aidan's first fall was not going to happen on my watch.

I gingerly maneuvered myself to a kitchen chair. Aidan couldn't have moved if he'd wanted to. His mother smiled at my accomplishment and mercifully offered to relieve me of my holding duties.

The experience lasted perhaps two minutes, but both Aidan and I survived my first encounter with exposure therapy, and I overcame a fear without a name. There would be hundreds more experiences holding Aidan and then the joy of catching him as he'd run and leap into my arms.

———

REASON #2 THE BIG GUY

✿ ✿ ✿

Most of us are given a nickname early in life. The source may or may not be identified. It is sometimes bestowed by a grandparent, an uncle or aunt, a sibling's mispronunciation, or even derived from parent's joy or frustration.

I'm not sure why during that first hospital visit with Aidan being in Mommy's arms I picked "The Big Guy" for Aidan Michael.

But I have rarely referred to Aidan by a name other than The Big Guy and his parents, Grammie and others have always used that nickname as well.

Aidan was a few months short of his third birthday. One day, upon his arrival at Grammie's house, he ran from the car, leaped into my arms, and I asked "How's 'The Big Guy?'"

Aidan looked at me as though he had heard something for the first time.

"Karl, why do you call me 'The Big Guy?'"

"Well, I've just always called you 'The Big Guy.'"

"But why?"

"Well, it's a nickname. Almost everyone has a nickname and we all just call you 'The Big Guy.'" That was the best I could do.

"I know. Grammie sometimes calls me 'The Big Guy' too. Is that OK?"

"Yes, Aidan, having a nickname is very common and we just like 'The Big Guy'."

"OK, Karl, but that's not a very good reason."

"Well, Aidan," I said with some frustration. "I call your little brother 'The Little Guy,' right? So you should be 'The Big Guy.'"

"Oh, now I understand," he said. "Evan is a little guy. I'm the big guy. Karl, do you have a nickname?"

"No, Aidan, I'm just Karl."

"Good, because you'll always be my best friend. Just Karl."

———

REASON #3 MOMMY WASN'T UPSET

✿ ✿ ✿

Aidan ready for a ride

Like all young kids, Aidan enjoyed his stroller rides with grandparents pushing. Aidan was always accompanied by his bear, his blanket and Bah — that colorful pacifier his parents preferred over thumb sucking.

The Bah was part of Aidan his first three years wherever we went … including frequent strolls with Karl.

Along our route several stops were mandatory, including peering down through the grid into the town's stormwater drainage system. Aidan loved to drop sticks and small stones into the drain and wait for the "kur-plunk."

I would hand Aidan little stones and he would lean over from the seat of the stroller, drop the stone, and listen for that splash. On this particular day, the unexpected happened. In his enthusiasm, that red Bah fell out of his mouth, dropped into the drain along with the stones, and was left floating in the drain.

"Karl, oh no!" Aidan screamed with tears in his eyes. "My Bah! My Bah! You have to get my Bah. Mommy is going to be really upset."

I explained the difficulty of retrieving the Bah; Aidan would have none of it.

"Karl, we *have* to get the Bah," he insisted. "Mommy said if I lost my Bah again there would **not** be a new one. That's what she said."

I assured him that Mommy would understand that it was an accident and there would be another Bah. "No, Karl, Mommy told me when I lost my green one that this was the last one."

"Aidan, let me explain it to Mommy. I'll tell her it was my fault," I offered. That's what grandpas are supposed to do, right?

"No, Karl, " Aidan insisted. "Mommy said to tell the truth and I'll tell her myself."

Arriving back at the house, Aidan marched into the house alone to explain the disaster to Mommy.

Minutes later he was back outdoors to report the results. With a sigh of relief, "Karl, we're OK. Mommy wasn't upset. She said it was an accident, that I didn't really lose the Bah. And guess what? Mommy said I'm getting a new *red* Bah."

And with that, Aidan gave me his recently learned "wink."

———

REASON #4 GRAMMIE, WATCH ME SHOVEL

✵ ✵ ✵

There are endless opportunities to teach grandkids work skills.

The snow began Friday night. By morning, a four-inch layer of fluffy flakes provided the first opportunity for Aidan to use his brand new snow shovel, one designed for a 3 1/2 year old.

Aidan was barely able to finish Grammie's waffles. In his eagerness to get outside, impatiently he struggled into his snowsuit, gloves, socks, boots, and hat. At 42 inches tall he grabbed his 36 inch shovel and headed out to help Grammie and Karl. He surveyed the vast white New Hampshire landscape and announced, "I'm going to shovel the whole driveway."

But how? Aidan was immediately confronted with a new learning experience. How do you use the shovel to move the snow? Still one year from the "I can do it myself" stage, Aidan opted to observe his grandparents' shoveling techniques.

Grammie is a traditionalist: she lifts a shovel load of snow and throws it, employing back, torso, and upper arms. My back favors a different approach: I push the snow using the shovel like a snowplow, then give the shovel a swift kick to clear the ever-growing scoop at the driveway's edge. After careful study, Aidan made his move.

Scooping a shovel full of white stuff, Aidan dramatically threw it to his left atop Grammie's growing snow pile. With equal flair, he turned and kicked his right foot high into the crisp morning air!

Three more scoops and throws – each followed by that little high-kicking right leg. Aidan had decided on a combination of the two techniques.

———

REASON #5 MADE PERFECT SENSE

✳ ✳ ✳

All grandparents and parents have received and given the command: "Take off your shoes!"

This instruction certainly ranks somewhere in the Top 10, along with "Don't talk with your mouth full" and "Brush your teeth."

Aidan had just turned two and was paying a visit to Uncle Brian's house with his parents for a family gathering. It was raining when they arrived and Aidan's father warned Aidan: "Your shoes are wet, so take them off before you step into Uncle Brian's house."

"I will Daddy," Aidan nodded.

Uncle Brian opened the door. Reaching the front porch, Aidan prepared to enter. He knelt down, pulled loose the velcro clasps on his shoes, stepped out of the shoes, reached over the threshold, and set them carefully onto the tiles of the entry floor. He then stepped back into his shoes, fastened the clasps, and ran to see his cousins.

When he caught up with him, his father commented, "Aidan, I told you to take your wet shoes off when you stepped into Uncle Brian's house."

"Daddy, I did," responded Aidan. "I took them off before I stepped into Uncle Brian's house. That's exactly what I did!"

Made perfect sense to Aidan … and to both his smiling father and Uncle Brian.

———

REASON #6 WINGS OF SONG

✧ ✧ ✧

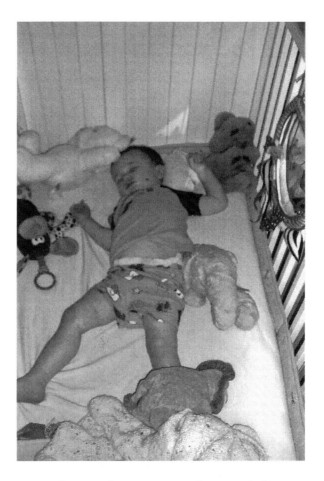

Another night courtesy of James Galway

It was by chance during a visit to Barnes and Noble that I elected to buy the CD *Wings of Song* featuring flutist James Galway. The soothing music had been playing over the store's sound system and once it was identified for me, I purchased two copies of the CD.

Mommy enjoyed music and Aidan was exposed to a variety of music. Mommy always played soft, soothing music at night while putting Aidan to bed. They would listen to soothing music while mommy murmured softly and Aidan drifted off to sleep.

Aidan was age two when I gave Mommy her copy of *Wings of Song*, suggesting this collection of peaceful compositions might be an option for his sleep time preparation. It soon became one of his favorites; in fact, a few of the songs became a prerequisite to assuring a quick escape to dreamland.

When Aidan visited, the floor in my office was one of his favorite play areas. Aidan especially enjoyed his access to my CD player, pressing the buttons to start it and selecting songs at random.

The music was generally in the background, and on one play afternoon, *Wings of Song* was in the player, and when Aidan pushed the play button, John Denver's "Annie's Song" filled the air. This brought Aidan to an immediate level of excitement only a two-year-old can show. "Karl! Karl! That's my song! That's what Mommy plays at night. That's my song!"

Aidan immediately dropped everything we were doing, curled up on the floor, and gave the order: "Karl, lie down," he said. "Lie down right here next to me. Close your eyes. It's time to go to sleep."

I did as told, but I needed more information. "Why do we have to go to sleep right now?" I whispered.

"Well," said Aidan in a hushed voice. "Mommy says that song is the last one before it's time to close our eyes and go to sleep."

And so for at least the next year during playtime in the office whenever that CD reached "Annie's Song," Aidan and I stopped whatever we were doing, and for the entire 2 minutes and 58 seconds "slept" on the office floor. We then picked up our game where we left off.

———

REASON #7 IT'S ALL ABOUT ME

✳ ✳ ✳

Just shy of age 5, Aidan would soon be headed for kindergarten. A preschool math book was one of Aidan's favorites. Being a believer that kids should learn math without the aid of computers and calculators, I was pleased each time he opened the book, even if for only 10 minutes.

Lying on my office floor absorbed in a page on patterns, Aidan had the opportunity to color a row of eight cars with his pattern of choice. I, of course, was looking for a red, red, blue, yellow, followed by a red, red, blue, yellow or some such combination.

Aidan chose to create a kaleidoscope of yellow, red, brown, blue, green, orange, purple, and blue. When I interrupted his labor and explained that he really was not making a pattern, he looked at me with that exasperated 'Karl, I know what I'm doing look,' and stated emphatically, "Karl, I can do it this way if I want to. *When I'm at Grammie's house, it's all about me.*"

I was startled. "Excuse me? It's all about you?"

"That's what Daddy said," Aidan replied without hesitation.

"I don't think so ..." I said.

"Yes he did," Aidan insisted. "Daddy said, 'when you're at Grammie and Karl's house it's all about you, but it is <u>not</u> that way when you're at home'."

———

REASON #8
WACKENMOCKENSNOCKER

✼ ✼ ✼

The bedtime story was a mandatory highlight of our sleepover routine. Fifteen minutes before it was time to close our eyes, Aidan and I would snuggle in Grammie's bed. Lights out and the regular request would come like clockwork. "Karl, tell me *that* story again."

The beginning and ending of the story was always the same. It was the timeline between fantasy and reality for a three-year old.

Once upon a time … the main character was "Wackenmockensnocker" who ventured out from his Grammie's house ("but not my Grammie's house" Aidan would insert), to join his friends in the woods ("but not my Grammie's woods" Aidan would insert). Wackenmockensnocker would often meet "Lucylockermootheroker" and "Sammyockenlockerstopper" and climb a hill and around the corner they would find "Terrytottersockenlucker" to engage in some kind of mischief.

Each time a new character would appear in the story, Aidan would laugh at each tongue-twisting name. The faster the names were spoken the louder the laughter. The story would end with characters returning to their homes and Wackenmockensnocker would hurry back to Grammie's house for milk and a snack before bedtime.

Aidan knew that when the story ended it meant real sleep time for him but always needed to be reassured. "Karl, I just want to be sure. That was not *my* Grammie's house, right?" My response was expected and it always gave him great comfort. "No Aidan, not *your* Gammie's house. Her house is just for you."

"Right, Karl. Now we can go to sleep."

———

REASON #9 ZINGERS

✵ ✵ ✵

One of the joys of spending time with your grandkids is catching the unexpected observations that make you chuckle.

- Admittedly some of them raise the ire of Mommy. For example, Aidan rolling his eyes and shaking his head with "whatever" when being corrected or told to do something not to his liking. Mommy's response is often a rather stern "Aidan, that's not how we answer." Unless it really mattered, my response was usually "Whatever to you, Aidan," and we'd exchange a wink or a smile.
- Or in the middle of a discussion with Aidan trying to explain something or find an immediate answer. Aidan liked "Karl, it's just not really relevant." *Just a four-year old being an adult.*
- Or Grammie having fixed a meal with ground beef, prompting Aidan to mention what he had learned in school. "Grammie, did you know that cows grow into beef?"
- Or Aidan showing me how to cut out paper snowflakes and Aidan noting my impatience to complete the project. "Karl, just wait. You need to watch and learn."
- Or as Aidan began to learn about the different states showing him a U.S. map and pointing out to him where my brothers Mick and Dave live. "Karl, why don't your brothers live together like Evan and me?"
- Or mentioning my mother whom Aidan never met. "Karl, you had a mother? You never told me."
- Or Karl insisting that we need to hurry or we'll be late. "Breathe Karl. Breathe." *Just a five-year old being an adult.*
- And perhaps Aidan's favorite response, especially when asked to do certain tasks or there is a need for an excuse. "I'm just a kid."

There is a fine line between innocent comments and being a smart aleck, and yes, parents need to police insolent remarks. But grandparents have more leeway and license.

REASON #10 THE ONE-ARMED MAN

✢ ✢ ✢

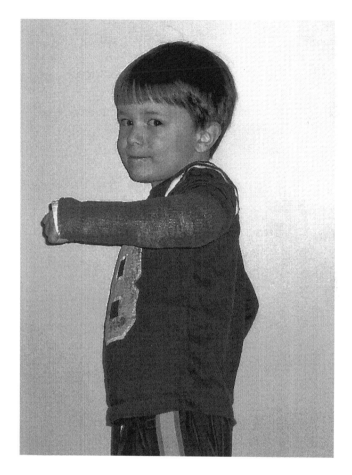

The aftermath of Aidan's unsuccessful attempt

There are several guarantees with little boys. They will run, jump, and climb — all leading to the inevitable visit(s) to the doctor's office or their first look at the bright lights of an emergency room. Aidan met his quota of visits, beginning with six stitches above his left eye before he was two.

Then at two and a half Aidan attempted to stand on a large exercise ball. He broke the three-foot fall with his left arm. The X-rays revealed a broken bone just above the wrist, which required a hand-to-elbow cast. The injury report was quickly e-mailed to family members.

Aidan visited us the next day sporting his bright red cast. He cheerfully provided a full account of the accident, and the trip to the doctor's office. "They were really nice and it didn't hurt while they made the cast for me. The doctor said it was a 'special cast' just for me."

I suggested to Aidan that he would have to be careful while wearing the cast so his arm would get better. "The doctor told me I can do anything I want, but I probably can't bat for a few days. He told Mommy that my arm would be 'better than new.' But it seems funny that breaking an arm makes it better than new. Why?" I had no response to his question.

"Did you ever break your arm, Karl?"

"A long time ago, Aidan, when I was about five years old."

"How did that happen?"

Not wanting to alarm him with the multiple ways that broken arms can occur, I opted for a safe answer. "I was playing ball with my brothers. We were jumping from one big kick ball to another when I slipped and landed on my left arm."

"Wow, just like me! Well, Karl, if you break it again, you can use my cast. I'll save it for you."

———

REASON #11
YOU WORRY TOO MUCH

✠ ✠ ✠

Monkey bars, swing sets, slides, jungle gym and teeter totters. Aidan loved the playground and like all kids he needed to master the equipment at his own pace. Each step of progress was a moment of pride for both Aidan and me.

But I repeatedly used the all-too-familiar grandparent warning, "Be careful. Be careful, Aidan. Be careful." I realized that an accident was part of learning, but decided it would happen on his parent's watch, not mine.

On this day Aidan decided it was his day to slide down the 8-foot high fireman's pole without help. His previous experiences with the pole involved my reaching up and holding him at his waist. Aidan stood on the platform and announced, "Karl, I can do this myself." I replied that I would help, and moved into a position to catch him. "Karl, step back, I can do it myself."

"OK, but be careful."

Aidan shook his head in exasperation. Hands on his hips, Aidan stared directly down at me and said emphatically, "Karl, you worry too much."

He leaped forward, grasped the pole and successfully completed the slide.

A high five and Aidan's broad 'I told you so' smile left me shaking my head as he raced to the curvy slide. He was right.

✠ ✠ ✠

YOUR STORIES

All grandparents (and parents) have stories about their grandkids. Sharing those is part of the reward of spending time with your grandkids. Readers are invited to email their stories to grammierules@gmail.com. Your story could be selected for the Second Edition of "Reasons To Spend Time With Your Grandkids."

REASON #12
NASCAR AND COUNTING

✫ ✫ ✫

Opportunities abound to influence their interests when grandkids spend time at Grammie's house without parents.

There are many who question the sanity of watching 43 cars drive 400 times around a mile track at speeds of 160 mph. But NASCAR fans argue differently, and explain that having a favorite driver is the key to enduring a five hour telecast.

With Karl being a Matt Kenseth fan, driver of the #17 Dewalt Ford Fusion, it was a foregone conclusion that he would quickly became Aidan's favorite too. Aidan would look for the #17 yellow car in each race. At age 3 1/2 Aidan could identify many of the others: #20 Tony Stewart, #48 Jimmie Johnson, #24 Jeff Gordon, and more. Aidan also quickly picked up that there are "good guys" and "bad guys" on the track. He soon learned that Kyle Busch, driver of the #18 car, was not a family favorite. He was a bad guy. Matt Kenseth was a good guy.

About this same time Aidan found pleasure in counting from one to 100. As often as anyone would listen he would demonstrate this skill. I noticed that Aidan enjoyed stopping after saying the number 17 and inserting the name Matt Kenseth during his count. Later, the sequence became just "15, 16, Matt Kenseth, 18, 19 etc."

One day, when demonstrating his counting skill for a neighbor, Aidan counted numbers 1 through 10 quickly and then continued "11, 12, 13, 14, 15, 16, **Good Guy, Bad Guy**, 19, 20…"

I was surprised and proud of his ingenuity.

———

REASON # 13 MOVE OVER PHIL MICKELSON

✡ ✡ ✡

On his third birthday, Aidan's favorite among more than 20 gifts was a left-handed plastic golf club and three yellow plastic golf balls.

His mother feared for the dining room china as Aidan displayed his swing in the house. I envied his initial swings. They included a full back-swing and a complete PGA-level follow-through.

The plastic driver was soon replaced by a Wilson. When Aidan was age 4, Santa delivered a golf bag, two irons and a putter. Aidan at age 5 was the youngest kid in a week-long summer golf camp.

An animated account of his first day occupied our evening walk. Aidan eagerly outlined the instructor's lesson.

"Karl, we did six things today with Mr. Rogers," said Aidan holding up one finger. "First, this is how you stand. Feet together, feet apart." Two fingers went up: "Second, this is the fan in the hand..." Three fingers kept me on track to understand the idea of the "body at one o'clock..." and on through number six.

After the walk, I got my driver and Aidan did another run through of his lesson and critiqued my form.

"Oh, and Karl. One more thing. Know what Mr. Rogers calls *my* driver?"

I tried to imagine. "No, Aidan, what does Mr. Rogers call your driver?"

"Mr. Rogers says *my* driver is the **BIG** dog. The **BIG** dog."

REASON #14 KARL, YOU'RE ...

✳ ✳ ✳

Many older readers will vividly recall Art Linkletter's TV variety show House Party and the popular segment "Kids Say the Darndest Things." Grandchildren routinely bring that show back to life for their grandparents. There are times when those "darndest things" are said in public-- and even folks who, after seven decades, have learned to cope with awkward situations find themselves with red faces.

Several years ago, I stopped putting my dentist's kids through college. Vanity was abandoned, bridges and partials were discarded, and a full set of nicely-crafted dentures were installed.

As denture wearers know, those 32 porcelains can become ill-fitting, forcing a return to the dentist's chair. That appointment, however, isn't always easy to schedule, and sometimes you just endure an awkward mouthful.

I was at least three months overdue for an "adjustment," my "Ss" sounded like "Zs" and the dentures were uncomfortable. Aidan was three months shy of his fourth birthday when we took a quick trip to the store.

Aidan was patient as we--and five other customers behind us--waited while the check-out clerk struggled to calculate the change from my $20 bill.

Aidan tugged at my shirt and whispered, "Karl, I have to tell you something."

"Speak up, Aidan," I responded. "I can't hear you. You don't have to whisper."

Aidan stepped back, folded his arms, and announced to all within hearing distance: *"Karl, you're drooling."*

Laughter erupted from the college co-eds to the elderly. A toddler in line with his dad innocently inquired, "Daddy, what's drooling?"

✳ ✳ ✳

YOUR STORIES

All grandparents (and parents) have stories about their grandkids. Sharing those is part of the reward of spending time with your grandkids. Readers are invited to email their stories to grammierules@gmail.com. Your story could be selected for the Second Edition of "Reasons To Spend Time With Your Grandkids."

REASON #15 WHY DO YOU TALK LIKE THAT?

☆ ☆ ☆

Frequent Friday or Saturday night sleepovers with Grammie and Karl made Aidan aware of our evening and morning rituals.

Following my early evening walk, I would shower before playtime with Aidan. If the activities were indoors, I had a habit of leaving my dentures in the bathroom and we would play until bedtime. My morning routine was similar. I'd leave the dentures behind while I enjoyed a cup of coffee and read the newspapers. Playtime would resume when Aidan awoke.

Aidan and I never had a problem communicating – I learned his toddler years "language" just fine. Aidan seemed to understand my speech regardless of the location of my dentures. Without the dentures diction suffers, the "s" sounds like a "z," and other words are, well, a bit different.

But one evening when Aidan was five he surprised me.

It was Halloween, and we had returned from trick or treating. Aidan was spending the night. Refreshed after my shower, I joined him in the sunroom where he was sorting candy. "What are your favorites?" I asked.

"I like them all, but Grammie said I can have only five pieces tonight." At least three were in his mouth.

"Right, and then you have to brush your teeth."

Suddenly he stopped sorting, gave me an intent puzzled look and asked, "Karl, why do you talk like that only after you shower and in the morning?"

———

REASON #16 TV AND KARL

✡ ✡ ✡

If you think about it, what Aidan observed and puzzled over was often perfectly logical. Finding a simple explanation for a two-year-old was the more difficult task.

One rainy afternoon we were all visiting in the sunroom. Aidan's Mommy turned on the TV and began to flip through the channels. She stopped at the local public access channel when she noticed a recent town council meeting replay was being broadcast. I was in my second three-year term on the town council.

"Aidan, look at what's on TV," Mommy suggested as she noted that Karl was being shown rambling on about nothing.

Aidan sat motionless and stared at the screen. He looked at Mommy, then turned to look ...in the same room at Karl.

"Mommy, that's Karl!" He looked bewildered. "Karl's in the TV. Karl, you're in the TV ... but you're here, too."

Aidan walked over to the TV, touched the screen. Then he glanced back at Karl.

"Karl, you're in the TV and you're here. Mommy?" Obviously confused, Aidan was shaking his head.

Mommy started with a basic explanation. "Aidan, you know how Karl goes to meetings, right? Well, Karl's meetings are on TV. And they tape them, like a movie, and then they show them over and over again."

"Oh ... I get it," said Aidan. "They make a movie of Karl's meetings so they can show them on TV when little kids are awake. Like Curious George, right?"

Mommy smiled. "Sort of like that, Aidan."

———

REASON #17 FIRST ROUND OF GOLF - LEARN THE RULES, KARL

✵ ✵ ✵

The week-long golf camp only stimulated Aidan's already avid interest in swinging the golf clubs. Divots in Karl's lawn were OK … but Daddy, Mommy, or I took him to the driving range whenever possible.

That summer it was time for Aidan's first real nine holes at the local country club. We did not expect a duplication of Tiger's first performance - who reportedly broke 90 at age three. But we shared Aidan's excitement as we checked in and loaded the golf bags on the two carts; Mommy and Daddy in one cart, Aidan and Karl in the second headed to the first tee.

Aidan's small bag had four left-handed clubs and a glove for each hand. Wearing a new, bright yellow collared shirt, slacks, a Matt Kenseth cap hat, and sneakers, Aidan was ready.

We parked the carts and waited for our tee time. Meanwhile, Aidan surveyed the landscape, watched the players ahead of us tee off, and then stretched as he had learned at golf camp.

He turned to me with a worried look. With his palms up and shaking his head, Aidan said solemnly, "Karl, "you can't play."

Mommy, Daddy and I were taken by surprise.

"Aidan, why can't I play?" I asked, puzzled.

"It's your shirt, Karl."

"My shirt?"

"Karl, you should know," said Aidan. "You can't play golf without a collared shirt. Your shirt doesn't have a collar, and Mr. Rogers, he's my golf teacher, he said you *must* wear a shirt with a collar when you play golf."

And then Aidan made his first round of golf memorable for grandpa.

———

REASON #18 FIRST ROUND
OF GOLF – PART II

✲ ✲ ✲

It was decided. Aidan would play the red tees with Mommy; Daddy and Karl would play the white tees.

Aidan took charge. "Mommy, it's ladies first," said Aidan authoritatively.

Aidan watched intently as Mommy (a decent golfer) topped that initial tee shot and the ball rolled short of the edge of the creek. "That's OK, Mommy. That's OK," observed Aidan in teacher-like fashion.

Aidan approached his first tee shot and stepped back. "Hold your head still and swing through," he reminded himself. That natural left-handed golf swing sent the ball past Mommy's first tee shot. Aidan expressed concerned. "That's OK, Mommy, you'll catch up!"

Aidan was provided some assistance during those first 9 holes. Fairway shots were always teed up … and his driver worked overtime on the par 4, 410-yard first hole. But only five more shots and Aidan was on the green, putting for a triple bogey. I had gone out of bounds twice and was also lying six on the green! Two putts later and two 8s should have been recorded. But Aidan's math prevailed of course as he dropped the second putt from 10 feet and joyfully exclaimed, "I got a birdie!" He was given a 3.

Recording the final score for each hole was left to Aidan's discretion. Forget the number of shots to reach the green, a 2-3 putt was usually called a birdie and a 3-4 putt was par. Why not, I asked myself. Any score was secondary to this experience.

The white tee for the 9th hole requires driving over a large pond filled with golf balls - and ducks hoping not be hit. The red tee was on the other side of the pond.

Daddy's tee shot soared over the pond and landed 260 yards out. Aidan stood on the back side of the tee watching intently. My first tee shot missed a duck, but found a home in the bottom of the pond. Aidan's excitement grew as my second tee shot cleared the hazard.

"Mommy, I'm going to hit from the white tees like Daddy and Karl," Aidan announced. He reached for his driver. Mommy then explained that it was an awfully long way over the water, but Aidan was adamant. "I can make it," he insisted.

After landing three balls in the water, Aidan was not discouraged. "I did what Karl did. Right, Mommy?"

"Yes, Aidan you did exactly what Karl did."

———

REASON #19 OLD PEOPLE DIE

✲ ✲ ✲

At some point grandkids will ask their grandparents about old age and dying. Aidan was no exception. What always amazes me is <u>when</u> a discussion of a new topic occurs.

We had finished bowling two games on an "Aidan Playday" when grandpa gets to substitute for the regular sitter. Heading into the Fun Center for a game of miniature golf, Aidan stopped abruptly and asked, "Karl, do all people die when they get old?"

I recovered and replied, "Yes, they do … when they get *really* old."

"You're not really old, yet, so that means you aren't going to die, right?"

"No, I have a long time …". Aidan interrupted. "But I don't want you to die. I don't want you to go away. I want you to live a long time with me."

"I will," I promised. Thankfully we were entering the Fun Center and I was hoping the focus would shift to miniature golf.

But at the same time I was curious why a subject he had never discussed before came up. "Why did you ask me about dying?"

"Well, because all of the guys in my Lego Star Wars game die sometimes and I don't want you to die."

"Aidan, that is just a video game. They are just animated characters and you can shoot them …"

"Right, and then they come back to life to play again. I want a blue ball for miniature golf."

———

REASON #20 T-BALL

✪ ✪ ✪

Aidan's Perfect Swing

Most grandparents experience a moment when they imagine their grandkid in the major leagues, on center court, or sprinting in the Olympics. I prefer images of a World Series seventh game and a grandson's ninth inning grand slam home run making World Series history.

However, that vision was quickly blurred at a T-ball game played by preschoolers.

When preschoolers are fielding and hitting, baseball rules are altered slightly to make it possible for a three-inning game to be completed in two hours, or before meltdowns occur. It was Game 2 of a rigorous six-week, 10-game schedule for preschoolers. Aidan had been swinging the bat and connecting with the ball since age two. Understanding baseball rules and actually playing a game---well, those pieces would take a little longer.

In Game 2, Aidan elected to play first base for one inning. To a T-baller, "playing" a base means standing directly on the base, but playing first base can mean extra action. All hit balls are fielded (eventually) and an attempt is made to throw to first. As Aidan took first base, Coach Scott demonstrated the "ready" position. He emphasized that when a ground ball is hit toward first, "you need to both catch the ball and touch first base."

"Remember," the coach reiterated, "Touch first base and catch the ball. You must do both – touch and catch." Aidan listened attentively.

The opportunity to execute occurred immediately as a slow-rolling grounder headed toward first base. Aidan drifted a foot off the base, turned, touched the base deliberately with his left foot, then raced off the base eight steps to his right and successfully fielded the ball. With the ball secure in his glove he turned to coach Scott, "I did it! I touched the base and caught the ball!"

A smiling coach Scott could only respond with a high five and "You did, Aidan. You did it."

Mommy and Daddy shook their heads, gave a thumbs up, and cheered. Aidan smiled as though he had hit that World Series home run.

———

REASON #21 I'LL TAKE THESE, KARL, OK?

✫ ✫ ✫

Story Hour at the local public library is a treat for kids, parents, *and* grandparents. This weekly opportunity is free, but sitting in a circle on the floor with your grandkid would be worth the price of admission.

Following the story and related art project, the hunt for books to take home begins.

The process of checking out books that must be returned is a bit confusing to a two- or three- year-old. It took several visits for Aidan to understand what *borrowing* books meant.

As he poured through the kids shelves, Aidan would create a stack rather quickly. I would suggest that we limit the selections to three books, but Aidan's "Karl, just one more" usually added up to 5 or 6 books being checked out.

One evening I needed to buy a birthday gift for Aidan's soon-to-be one year old brother, and I invited Aidan, who had recently turned age three, to go with me to Barnes and Noble. Arriving at the store, I took him to the large kids section.

"Karl this is just like the library," Aidan observed as he flipped through an animal book. "Only know what, Karl? They have even more books."

Aidan worked his way through the preschool section of books for 3-5 year olds. I stood about 10 feet away to watch Aidan out of the corner of my eye while selecting a kid's picture book. Aidan was comfortable sitting on the floor and was thoroughly engrossed looking at the books.

Stepping back to Aidan's corner I probably should not have been surprised at what I found. Aidan had a stack of 10 new books in front of him. "Aidan, what are you doing with all those books?" I asked.

Aidan put one hand on the stack while pulling another colorful title off the shelf. "Well, I just need this one more and then I'll be ready to check out my books and go back to Grammie's house," he said. He placed it on the pile and said with satisfaction, "I'll take these, Karl, OK?"

———

REASON #22 THE GIRL IN WHITE

✠ ✠ ✠

Just before his first week of kindergarten, Aidan and his parents were scheduled to attend the orientation. With anticipation, I awaited Aidan's full report after the session. He didn't disappoint.

"Karl, guess what I did tonight?" There was no time to respond. "I went to school!"

"Wow, tell me …." The story rapidly unfolded…

"Mommy and Daddy took me and guess what? I had my own chair, we sit at a little table, I know two boys, and guess what, I had my own name tag and my own cubby." Aidan took a breath.

"You had your own cubby," I inserted, not really wanting to interrupt his account of the experience.

"Yes, but it wasn't very big."

"Were there boys and girls in your class?" I asked.

"I think so, but I only knew Jayson and Bryce. We played T-ball together, remember?

"And know what, Karl? They had a playground, but only two slides. And I met Mrs. Delatore. She's my teacher and really nice. She gave me my own book to take home and Mommy and Daddy are going to read it to me right now."

For the tenth time I managed to get in "That's great…" but as with most of Aidan's story-telling conversations, there was one more thing.

"And know what, Karl? There was this girl who came into my room and she was dressed all in white."

That observation took me by surprise. "So, this girl in white. She's in your class?"

"No, no, Karl. The girl in the white … she's the boss of the whole school. Mommy says she is the *big boss*."

─────

REASON #23 I STARTED SCHOOL YESTERDAY …

✷ ✷ ✷

It was late June. Aidan and I were taking a break from playing baseball. Sitting outside I elected to sit downwind from Aidan and lit up one of my favorite Erick cigars.

As he often does, Aidan caught me by surprise. "Karl, why do you put that fire in your mouth?"

During the past few years, few questions had been asked about those "things," but never this directly. My smoking habit was a subject usually reserved for annual discussions only with my physician. But I needed to answer Aidan.

"It is not a good idea," I said emphatically. "In fact, it is not something you should ever even think about doing."

From the puzzled look on his face, I knew more was coming. "So why do you do it?" asked Aidan. "If it's not a good idea, Mommy would say to stop. So why don't you stop?"

There are many options when answering questions from grandkids. With an uncomfortable question the option most often taken is the one that hopefully ends the discussion. I elected a short answer.

"Mommy is right," I said. "If it's a bad idea then you definitely should stop. So I am going to quit when you start school." His first day of kindergarten was almost three months away. I figured ….

That first day of school fell on a Wednesday. Aidan visited on Thursday. Taking a break from throwing the football, Aidan ran to the house for a drink. When he returned, he stopped short, set down his drink, and watched the Erick smoke drift into the woods.

He then jabbed his finger toward the smoke and said pointedly, "**Karl, I started school yesterday**."

———

REASON #24 THAT FIRST PICK UP

✧ ✧ ✧

Aidan ready for his first day of Kindergarten

It was Aidan's second day of kindergarten. *Don't be late.* Those were my instructions, given several times by Aidan's parents and Grammie as I prepared for my first "pickup." I was told to be in the school lobby at exactly 11:30 a.m. to meet Aidan.

I left home at 11:00 for the 10 minute ride, entered the building at 11:15, and verified with the receptionist that I really was "Karl to pick up Aidan." Next I was buzzed into the school rotunda where I could be watched while I waited. Within five minutes another 12 adults arrived.

At exactly 11:20 a group of five-year olds marched down a long hallway to the entrance of the rotunda. The students were instructed to walk directly to the adult picking them up and then turn and make eye contact with the teacher. I was impressed with the concern for safety exhibited by the staff.

As all the connections were made, I experienced panic. No Aidan! He was not with the group. I had questions needing immediate answers. Did I have the wrong building? The wrong school? The wrong time?

Only one other adult was still standing with me. I worried that perhaps Aidan had been lost, expelled, or snatched. He laughed and explained that another group would be coming momentarily. He had been through the drill the previous year with a daughter and was now waiting for his son, and there was more than one kindergarten class.

Still concerned and feeling only slightly better, another group of adults filed in and finally at 11:29 a second group of 12 children trooped in. The teachers again explained the routine to their charges and I breathed a sigh of relief when spotting Aidan third in line.

Spotting me, our faces broke into smiles simultaneously. He quickly pointed to me for his teacher who gave her blessing to leave. Aidan totally ignored the "walk to" instructions and with Olympic speed he raced and leaped into my arms.

"Did you have a good day?" I asked.

"Karl, it was awesome. **Awesome**. Now can we play miniature golf?"

Mission accomplished.

REASON #25 PRINCESS LEI-A

✵ ✵ ✵

Only the audience changes as Star Wars continues to lure new recruits and broaden its fan base. The characters, the story line, the magical effects never change -- especially the characters. Aidan at age five joined the new generation of Star Wars fans.

Star Wars became a favorite game to play, especially after Grammie bought light sabers that flashed red and blue. There were constant battles with Darth Vader and the "bad guys." And a length of clothesline strung in the birch tree at Grammie's allowed Luke Skywalker to swing down the hill gracefully carrying Princess Leia on his back.

In one simulated game, I was Princess Leia and Aidan was Luke Skywalker.

I wanted to double-check. "Aidan, I'm Princess Leah (Lee-ah), right?" I asked.

"Karl, I've told you before. You are Princess Leia (Lay-a). It's Leia (Lay-a), not Leah (Lee-ah)."

"OK."

"Karl, let's be sure," Aidan said with concern. "Repeat after me. Prin-cess… Lei-a. OK?

Now you say it."

"Prin-cess Lei-a," I repeated confidently, pronouncing each syllable distinctly.

"OK, you got it. Now get on my back and I'll swing you to safety."

———

REASON #26 WHAT MOMMY TEACHES

✢ ✢ ✢

A phone call from your grandkid – especially to relate a new experience – is one of the few times you actually appreciate hearing your house phone ring. Aidan's first several weeks of kindergarten produced many such calls.

They usually started with "Karl, guess what I did today?" … and I usually never had a chance to ask "what?"

"Well, today I did something new and different," said Aidan. "I went to a class that Mommy teaches at her school, but not at my school."

"And what class was that?" I asked.

"Well, today we had **P and E.**"

✢ ✢ ✢

YOUR STORIES

All grandparents (and parents) have stories about their grandkids. Sharing those is part of the reward of spending time with your grandkids. Readers are invited to email their stories to grammierules@gmail.com. Your story could be selected for the Second Edition of "Reasons To Spend Time With Your Grandkids."

REASON #27 MORE ZINGERS

✫ ✫ ✫

- Aidan would often find me "resting" on the living room sofa. He had frequently heard Grammie's comment about not playing (or sleeping) on the sofa. Aidan called it "Karl's favorite napping spot." After I injured my back, however, I discovered that lying on the sofa only aggravated the pain. Observing my changed behavior, Aidan inquired, "Karl, why don't you sleep on the sofa anymore?" I explained how it bothered my back. He smiled and winked. "I'll bet Grammie's happy because now you're following her rules, too."

- We pulled into a gas station and I said, "Hey, Aidan, take a look at that limousine." His response: "Wow, they must have a really big family, Karl."

- Aidan and I had spent the afternoon hitting a bucket of golf balls at the driving range. That evening Aidan and Grammie were watching a golf tournament on TV. "Look, Aidan," said Grammie. "That player hit the ball 214 yards to the green on a par 3 hole. Karl said you hit one 120 yards today. I bet when you're older you'll be able to hit it 200 yards." Aidan gave Grammie that let-me-understand-this look. "Does that mean when I'm really old I'll be able to hit it 1,000 yards?"

- Aidan and three-year old brother Evan were invited to spend a day with Grammie. The previous night, during a brief brotherly exchange, Aidan had bloodied Evan's nose. As she dropped off the boys, Mommy warned that such behavior would not be tolerated at Grammie's house. Such misbehavior would result in swift punishment. A first offense would mean a 5-minute time out. A second infraction would result in a 10-minute time out. A third would – heaven forbid - require the offender to spend one hour in a room by himself. Aidan listened silently and sighed. Then with a woeful expression on his face turned to Grammie. "Know what, Grammie? Know what? One hour is 60 minutes. Sixty *whole* minutes."

- A game of bean bag toss involved Grammie and neighbor girl Taryn on one team and Aidan and I on the other. I cheered when Grammie made a 10-point toss. "Karl, you can't cheer for Grammie. We're playing *versus*."

- Aidan enjoyed our neighbor Dave, who appeared frequently at Grammie's to help deal with a problem around the house. One day Aidan and Grammie were playing Frisbee. The game ended when the red Frisbee landed in a white birch tree. There it stayed, hanging from a branch about 30 feet above the ground. Grammie and Aidan tried unsuccessfully to knock the Frisbee free by tossing a ball at it. A frustrated Aidan finally was defeated and stopped. He thought for a minute, and then announced the solution. "Grammie, since we can't get it down, I guess we need to do what Karl does when there's a problem. Just call Dave."

———

REASON #28 WHAT'S A DRILL?

✵ ✵ ✵

Part-time retirement and part-time work means that grandparents are readily available for part-time child care "assignments" at the request of the grandkid's parents. On each assignment, Aidan usually asked early, "Karl, what are we going to do special today?" Mini-golf was among frequent first choices.

One of the assignments (for which I admittedly volunteered) was to pick Aidan up from kindergarten on Friday, a half-day of school. Early in the school year after Aidan leaped into my arms upon release, I suggested he say good-bye to his teacher Mrs. Delatore. Aidan returned, gave her a hug and said good-bye for the week-end. Mrs. Delatore walked over as Aidan returned. "Aidan was fine with the fire drill, today," she whispered. She had been alerted by Aidan's mother of Aidan's fear of fire. I told her that was great news and I'd certainly let his mother know.

The drive to mini-golf was a non-stop review of his 4-hour kindergarten morning and experiences – drawing, coloring, numbers … and then he got to the blow-by-blow of the fire drill. He explained how they all marched outside, but there wasn't **really** a fire. There were details about the noise level, the rule about standing quietly, and the orderly return to their room. Knowing how frightened and concerned Aidan was about anything related to fire, I breathed a sigh of relief.

Aidan finished his delightful account of the morning as we arrived at the mini-golf course. He was so satisfied with the fire drill experience, I thought that was over.

But . . . he had one more question. "Karl, what's a drill?"

I chose my words carefully. It means a practice just in case …but Aidan interrupted, nodding his head impatiently. "OK. I got it. Let's get a hole-in-one."

———

REASON #29 I DON'T KNOW HER NAME

✵ ✵ ✵

Aidan's fear of buses had been present since he was age two. To Aidan the bus was big, noisy, and without seat belts – a vehicle he once told me he won't ride until he was age 10.

"Guess what, Karl. We're going on a field trip next week to pick apples and, guess what; we're going to ride the bus."

I was a bit surprised at the excitement in his voice.

On field trip day I picked up Aidan for the short drive to school. "We're going on a field trip today … and we're taking the bus," he reminded me.

Aidan seemed deep in thought as we approached the school. "Karl, I'm just a little bit nervous," he said in a small voice. I reminded him about his trip to Six Flags where he experienced scarier rides in a whirling, noisy tea cup. "Right, I was big nervous then and only a little bit nervous now. I'm OK."

I wondered during the day about Aidan's bus experience. The answer came in a 5 pm call. "Karl, guess what? I rode the bus today." I heard excitement in his voice.

"That's great. Was it fun? Where did you sit?"

"Well, I sat next to the window on the way to Butternut Farm, and know what? A girl sat next to me."

"That's great. And what was her name?"

"Well, I don't know her name. *But she was a girl.*"

———

REASON #30 SEPTOBER 1, 2009

✫ ✫ ✫

You cannot underestimate the fun of watching a grandkid learn …

Aidan had finished week three of kindergarten and he was learning the months and days.

"Karl, know what day it is?" became a common question. Without waiting for an answer Aidan would continue, "Today is September 10, 2009."

"Karl, know what day it is? Today is September 12, 2009."

We had worked our way through the month of September when Aidan arrived for a sleepover on the first night of October. The important recurring question was asked. "Karl, know what day it is?"

"What day is it, Aidan?"

"Well, Karl, today is **Septober 1, 2009.**"

———

REASON #31 MAKE THAT NOISE AGAIN …

✵ ✵ ✵

Little boys rarely tire of hitting a baseball. "Karl, let's play baseball." The request could occur at anytime and Aidan knew the answer would always be "yes," regardless of the weather.

Aidan batted left-handed. His swing was natural and good at age two. At age three he made regular contact with the ball. By age four, with each long hit, he would ask, "Karl, is that a home run?"

The most used playing field was our wide long driveway. Home runs were reserved for balls hit deep into the woods, over small trees, or onto the roof of the house.

Announcements were part of each batting practice. When Aidan was younger, Grammie acted as the public address announcer. "Now batting cleanup, the homerun champion … AIDAN!"

By the time he was four, I assumed the announcer's role. My running commentary became longer and more detailed. "Now batting, the home run champion Aidan … Aidan will need a home run … the pressure is on the greatest home run hitter … it is for the world championship … Aidan must hit a home run and not get strike three … he must hit a home run!" I would then produce the sound of a loud cheering crowd, which Aidan loved. With a look of determination, he would tap his bat on the chalk-drawn home plate and await the next pitch.

During one particularly long "game," we had gone through several introductions, and several home runs, and a couple of strikeouts - but Aidan always got another chance to win the championship. After another long introduction, Aidan swung and missed twice. Just as I was prepared to pitch, Aidan stepped back from the plate and rested the bat on his shoulder.

"Karl, you know I have two strikes and I need to hit a home run. Make that loud noise again. Make more noise!"

The "crowd" cheered loudly. Aidan hit the next pitch and it was called a home run, of course.

———

REASON #32 NO HOME DEPOTS

✳ ✳ ✳

Forget the history books. Real history is explained by 5-year-olds.

"Karl, know what we talked about today in school?" This common opening question from Aidan never really required an answer as he delved right into the subject. "Well, we studied Thanksgiving Day and the Pilgrims."

"Here's what happened," said Aidan with the confidence of a narrator on a PBS historical documentary. "The King of England wouldn't let the pilgrims go to church so they got on a boat with sails and came to this country so they could go to church."

"But when they got here, guess what? There was no Basket Market to buy groceries so they had to grow their own," explained Aidan with a tone of concern. I suppressed a smile, sure that the stockholders in the "Market Basket" grocery chain would understand.

"But there was another problem," said Aidan, his arms apart, palms up and a look of desperation on his face. "They didn't have any houses. No houses. And know what, Karl? There were no Home Depots either."

———

REASON #33 MOMMY
SHARES A GRANDKID STORY

✫ ✫ ✫

Aidan and Mommy

Grandparents love phone calls from their children to share stories about their grandkids. And each one is worth listening to.

As Aidan's fifth Christmas approached, Daddy had taken him shopping for Mommy's present.

Then came the excitement of hiding the present until Christmas day. Daddy and Aidan decided that a large metal cabinet in the basement garage would be the perfect spot to stash the gift. Daddy explained that it was not a cabinet Mommy ever used.

Three days before Christmas while Mommy was buckling Aidan's younger brother in the car, Aidan suddenly noticed the hiding spot for Mommy's presents.

Walking over to the metal cabinet, Aidan said with alarm, "Mommy, if you need something in there, don't get it."

"Why Aidan?" Mommy could see the wheels spinning in Aidan's head as he searched for a plausible reason.

"Because there is dangerous stuff in there."

Mommy was immediately curious about the "dangerous" stuff. "Like what, Aidan?"

"Bees, Mommy. Bees."

Struggling not to laugh, Mommy remained serious. "Aidan, is that where you and Daddy hid my Christmas present?"

"Yeah ... we bought it at the Christmas Dove, but I can't tell you."

————

REASON #34 ANOTHER MOMMY STORY

✵ ✵ ✵

With kids come guarantees - skinned knees and elbows, colds, tummy aches and more. Guaranteed.

Aidan, of course, had his share.

Aidan's school schedule included full days Monday and Wednesday and a half-day Friday. It was his second week of school and Aidan had a tummy ache on one of his off days but started to feel better that night. Putting him to bed, Mommy commented "I hope you feel better in the morning so you can go to school."

"If I'm not better do I have to stay home?" Aidan asked with concern.

Mommy explained that would be the proper procedure so as not to spread germs and make others sick.

Aidan was anxious. "But, Mommy, will I get in trouble if I don't go?"

"Absolutely not. Mrs. Delatore would want you to stay home and get better."

Aidan pondered that explanation for a moment. "Well, will you let her know I'm not coming?"

"I definitely will call the office and tell them you won't be there."

Another pause. Aidan wanted to be sure all was taken care of.

"OK, Mommy. That's fine. But will you email Mrs. Delatore a message so she knows, in case they forget to tell her? I don't want her to *worry* where I am."

✵ ✵ ✵

YOUR STORIES

All grandparents (and parents) have stories about their grandkids. Sharing those is part of the reward of spending time with your grandkids. Readers are invited to email their stories to grammierules@gmail.com. Your story could be selected for the Second Edition of "Reasons To Spend Time With Your Grandkids."

REASON #35 AGONY OF VICTORY

✵ ✵ ✵

Kids and water. Some learn to swim as naturally as they first learned to crawl.

For others, the words fear and the pool are synonymous.

Aidan fit the latter category.

Aidan had eight private swimming lessons during the winter at age four. The lessons appeared to provide him some comfort in the water.

However, that summer while swimming at an outdoor pool, Aidan slipped and found himself on the pool's bottom. He surfaced unharmed, but the fear of water and the pool resurfaced as well.

A few more tries failed to eliminate or even reduce his fear.

Eight more private lessons were booked for the fall. Fortunately Amy, the instructor, had a full understanding of the challenge. She spent the first two week's gaining Aidan's trust. There were constant negotiations. For example, Amy would suggest 30 seconds floating, Aidan would say "how about 10?"

Finally, it was week 8. Amy elected to give an extended lesson. She was determined to win this battle. And she did. Aidan kicked and paddled the entire length of the pool with the noodle while Amy crawled along side to avoid another sinking setback.

But there was one more challenge and Amy was determined to be the winner. Aidan was instructed to hold on to the side of the pool and then to push away and swim 4-5 yards to her. Aidan had a worried, frightened look on his face. He refused to let go and swim to Amy. The minutes seemed like hours as Amy encouraged him, pleaded, and assured him that he could do it.

I sat helplessly by feeling badly for both of them. After an eternity Aidan let go and executed eight strokes to reach Amy's waiting arms. He then swam back to the edge of the pool and gave me big thumbs up.

Back at Grammie's house Aidan recounted the tale of his success. A triumphant call to Mommy was made. "I did it. Mommy, I did it," reported Aidan excitedly. "I swam the *length of the pool all by myself.*"

Later, I drove Aidan to his house. As we pulled into the driveway, Aidan said, "Karl, I'm really sad."

"You're sad? Why?"

"Because I can't go swimming tomorrow. I want to swim every night."

———

REASON #36 GRAMMIE'S RULES

✷ ✷ ✷

Sleepovers produce experiences as enjoyable for grandparents as they are for grandkids. Aidan never disappointed.

Six weeks short of his sixth birthday, Aidan did what all boys tend to do at that age. Acting like Curious George, he was in the sun room swinging and jumping from chairs to the sofa. My first two requests fell on deaf ears. The activity finally ended with my third request.

"Karl, why did you tell me to stop swinging," said Aidan with a sober look on his face. "Is that a Grammie rule?"

I responded quickly and firmly. "No Aidan, that is a Karl rule."

"Well, then it was OK that I didn't stop. Because Daddy said that when I am at Grammie's house I have to follow Grammie's rules."

———

REASON #37 CATTAILS

✦ ✦ ✦

On Fridays, picking up Aidan at 11:30 pm from kindergarten was on my schedule. Although the afternoon activities varied, the first stop was always McDonald's for a Happy Meal.

The parking lot at our local McDonald's abuts a swamp and wetlands, resulting in a wonderful stand of cattails, that water-loving plant with a brown, hot dog shaped cone on the top.

Every child needs to experience breaking open a cattail and watching the literally hundreds of light, fluffy seeds float away.

Aidan was no exception. After Karl would sink in the mud cutting the cattails, Aidan loved waving them in the air. "We need to help more cattails grow," he observed.

It was on our third October adventure with cattails that Aidan decided he wanted to take cattails home to Mommy and Daddy, brother Evan, and one for Grammie, too. Following Aidan's directions I picked four of the largest and then loaded both Aidan and the cattails into the back seat.

"Aidan, remember, little white fluffy seeds fly all over when you break open the cones – they are **not** to be opened in the car," I instructed.

"Right, Karl. I just hope they don't break open."

There was a lot of traffic requiring my attention and Aidan was unusually quiet as we drove to Grammie's house. Suddenly he broke the silence. "Karl, can you put down the back window? I *think* I broke a cattail open."

Within seconds of the window rolling down, winter in October exploded within the car. Aidan also was having visibility issues. His solution was to hold the broken tails up directly in the wind now blowing into the back seat … and the car was a whiteout.

Somehow we arrived safely at Grammie's house. I opened Aidan's door quite speechless and unsure how to react. He and the car were both covered in white fluff.

But Aidan had the situation in hand.

"Karl, I think you were right," said Aidan. "I just wish they hadn't broken open. And we need to be more careful when you put down the window. But I have an idea. Let's get the leaf blower."

———

REASON #38 GOING GREEN

✳ ✳ ✳

"Karl, the can."

"Karl, the bottle."

"Karl, the paper."

"Karl, turn off the water."

OK. I know that individuals should make environmental concerns a personal concern. But I confess that my habits of multiple decades were not easily broken - until Aidan decided he had seen enough of Karl destroying the environment.

It began while brushing teeth. Three-year old Aidan repeatedly turned off the water while brushing. He explained, "Karl, *you* need to do this. There is only so much water in the whole world and Mommy says we need to save it. *You* must always turn off the water when not using it. I'm going to tell Grammie too."

With Aidan around, there were constant reminders about separating cans and bottles and putting papers aside. When he wasn't around I felt guilty sneaking a can into the daily trash!

Once he reached kindergarten, all of these concerns were reinforced with readings and projects, including reminders and observations of recycled materials. Outdoor environmental Issues were added to the list – using leaves for garden compost and lawn watering.

When I needed to trim branches from a tree hanging overhanging the driveway, Aidan expressed concern. "Karl, are you sure those branches will grow back and the tree won't die?"

I wanted to tell him that it was only a scrub tree and that I really <u>wanted</u> it to die … but I didn't. "Yes, Aidan, the branches will grow back and the tree will survive," I assured him.

"Good," he said waving his little arm expansively toward the densely forested acres next to the house. "That's what we need to save."

———

REASON #39 ALIENS, REALLY

✩ ✩ ✩

Grandparents who have had the privilege of picking up their grandkids from school, especially during the early years, understand why every possible effort is made not to miss this opportunity. Their comments and observations about the day's experiences are, well, precious.

Aidan never disappointed.

Every Friday at 11:30 am following our pick-up routine, I would secure Aidan in the car seat and wait for his question, "Karl, what are we going to do special today?"

This particular Friday was different. Instead of the usual question, Aidan was bursting with excitement. "Karl, something *really* big happened today!

"You know my friend Bryce, right?" said Aidan. "Well guess what Bryce saw today? Bryce saw an alien. A real live alien."

"A live alien. There is no such thing, Aidan," I replied. "That is just fiction. It's make-believe."

"No, Karl. Bryce did see an alien. He saw it near the woods during recess. He really did."

"Aidan, there are no aliens," I said firmly. "I think Bryce just made it up. You only see aliens in movies or video games like Star Wars."

"Yes, there *are* aliens, Karl," Aidan insisted. "Bryce saw it. I didn't see it because Bryce said it flew away in its space ship. And I know that Bryce is not a liar."

"I know that your friend Bryce wouldn't lie, but ...".

"OK. OK. I want to see it too and when I do then I'll tell you about it," replied Aidan. "Then you'll know it *is* true. And guess what we did in music class today?"

———

REASON #40 MOMMY, BIGGEST FISH EVER

✵ ✵ ✵

Tom Sawyer. Huck Finn. Norman Rockwell. Images of the little boy and his fishing pole are part of being … well, being a boy. And little boys waste little time learning to tell fish stories just like grown men.

At his third Christmas, Aidan received a plastic fishing pole allowing him to "cast" a rubber worm throughout the house. Parents and grandparents frequently forget that "waiting" to play with gifts is not part of Christmas.

We discouraged ice fishing through the winter and finally a warm spring day sent us to the town pond. Preparation was predictable. Aidan dug into Karl's most fertile lawn spot newly planted with grass seed to find bait (and play with the worms). We survived a fish hook in Aidan's clothing.

To avoid disappointment, I cautioned Aidan that it was unlikely we would catch a fish on our first try. I was sure nothing larger than a very small sunfish had ever been caught in that pond.

Aidan was not so sure. "Karl, we'll catch one. A really big one," he assured me as I cast the line 20-feet out and handed Aidan the pole. A 30-second wait then Aidan suggested "maybe the fish are over there." A second cast. The bait slipped off a lily pad and I handed the rod to Aidan.

Suddenly the bobber disappeared, the line reeled out, and the pole bent forward. I grabbed the pole with a jerk and a 14-inch small mouth bass actually leaped into the air. I turned to hand the pole back to Aidan, but the leaping fish and my grabbing of the pole scared him and he had run back to the car.

Aidan nervously crept back to observe my clumsy efforts to remove the hook. "Karl, don't hurt him – don't hurt him!" We finally released him unharmed back into the pond.

When we arrived back at Grammie's house, Mommy was waiting.

"Mommy, it was this big," said Aidan with outstretched arms. "This big. Biggest fish ever!"

"Did you catch him?" asked Mommy. She waited for Aidan to catch his breath.

"Well, Karl helped. But we caught him and then gave him back to his mommy and daddy and brother."

———

REASON #41 MORE GRANDKID STORIES

☆ ☆ ☆

Mommy and Daddy were driving back with Aidan and little brother Evan from a visit at their great-grandmother's (Grammie Kay) house.

"Mommy, why do we have hearts?" Aidan asked.

"They make our bodies work," said Mommy. "Kind of like batteries in toys that make toys work."

"OK, well are heart attacks real?"

"Yes, they're real," said Mommy. She was unsure where this was going. "When people are old sometimes their heart doesn't work as well and they have to have a doctor fix it. Aidan, where did you hear about heart attacks?"

"Well, Grammie Kay said that their cat was going to have a heart attack."

Daddy elected to join in. "Aidan, that's just an expression. Sometimes grownups say something that's just pretend - like if someone is bothering you, you might say 'go jump in the lake' ... you really don't want them to jump in the lake, you just want them to leave you alone. Sometimes grownups say things that are really confusing."

"Yeah, 'cause I'm only a little kid," concluded Aidan.

Evan had been listening quietly but now joined in the conversation. "I'm afraid of bears."

Surprised at the non sequitor, Mommy explained that bears live in the woods and there is no need to be afraid.

Aidan was back in the conversation. "Mommy, what if they come in our house?"

"Our dog Jackson wouldn't let them in the house, he'll protect us," said Daddy.

Aidan needed more. "Well, what if Jackson's heart didn't work and he died?"

Mommy reassured him. "We take good care of Jackson and he'll live with us for a long time.

"But if he dies, it's OK to be sad, but we'll think about getting a new pet."

Not enough for Aidan. "Well, what if that one dies?"

"Then we'll get a new one."

"But Mommy, what if that one dies too?"

Exasperation was setting in. "We'll get another new one," Mommy replied.

Thankfully Evan rejoined the exchange with "I'm hungry."

"Me too," said Aidan.

———

REASON #42 ONE
FOR THE MUSEUM

✳ ✳ ✳

One can surmise that some of the early cave paintings were probably the handiwork of kids. Why not? Drawing, coloring, and painting are favorite pastimes of all kids and certainly offer a delightful and rewarding activity for grandparents and grandkids to share.

Aidan's early drawings – those colored lines that zigzag across the page, their meaning known only to him – are saved in "Aidan's box" at Grammie's house. This artwork one day will bring smiles to both Aidan and mommy.

As with all four-year-olds, Aidan's venture into painting required numerous brushes and the joy of mixing colors. Aidan called it "making new colors."

One rainy weekend we elected to practice the art of finger painting. Aidan loved it. Gobs of paint, no brushes and frequent adult praise for just making a mess.

Aidan finished almost two dozen 6" by 9" works of art and spread them on newspapers to dry. Imagination ran rampant as Aidan and I identified what we saw in each piece – everything from animals to monsters.

Admiring his work, Aidan asked, "Karl, what are we going to do with all these paintings?"

I suggested we put his favorites in stand-up, clear plastic desk frames and give one to Mommy and Daddy, Grammie, and brother Evan. Aidan's distribution list soon grew to include 10 people.

"Mommy and Daddy can put them on their desks at work and show people they work with," said Aidan. "And if the other people like them, we can give them more."

I concurred that it was a great idea … but Aidan had a question.

"Karl, what happens to a painting that a lot of people really like?"

I explained that really good paintings are often placed in art museums where many people can appreciate them.

"I like that idea," said Aidan. "Then everybody can see them."

Aidan gestured toward his array of paintings. "Karl, which one is your favorite?"

I identified my selection. Aidan turned it around several times, looked at me, studied his work further, and then nodding his head approvingly, "Karl, this is the one for everybody to see. This one I'll give to the museum."

———

REASON #43 CHANGE YOUR SHIRT, MURRAY

✵ ✵ ✵

At an early age, Aidan found joy in music of all genres. Classical and piano music at bedtime and sing-a-long folk music at Grammie's house. Even in the car he had his favorites, begging "Mommy, play that one again."

I suspect my parents and grandparents shook their heads at the Everly Brothers, the Kingston Trio and Ricky Nelson. But every generation has many choices and one of Aidan's was an Australian group named The Wiggles. It required a long time for Karl to understand the words and, equally important, the dress code.

My first exposure to the four Aussies and their Big Red Car was a live concert with three-year old Aidan and Mommy. Aidan joined several hundred others laughing, singing, and grooving in the aisles.

After that, playing The Wiggles CDs at Grammie's house became a group activity. Everyone in the room was required to dance (jump, run, and fall down) to "Hot Potato," "Shaky Shaky," "Fruit Salad," and Aidan's favorite "Come On, Let's Jump" -- I liked "D.O.R.O.T.H.Y. (My Favorite Dinosaur)."

And there were numerous opportunities to "play The Wiggles" as Aidan identified another of his invented games.

As fans of The Wiggles know, Anthony wears a blue shirt, Greg yellow, Murray red, and Jeff purple.

Aidan identified the roles at the start of each "game." "Karl, you'll be Murray with your red shirt on and I'll be Greg since my shirt is yellow." We would then play and dance to The Wiggles' tunes and talk to both Jeff and Anthony pretending they were in the room.

Aidan would decide when we needed the other band members "live." "Karl, you go change your shirt to purple and I'll put on my blue jacket and then Jeff and Anthony can play." Of course grandpa complied. This was just plain fun.

Playtime ended when Mommy arrived for pickup. A worn-out Karl carried the still lively Aidan to the car. "Ok, Aidan, I'll see you tomorrow," I said, kissing him goodbye.

"Jeff, Aidan's not here. I'm Anthony, remember? "

"Oh right," I replied. I'd already forgotten character. "See you tomorrow, Anthony."

"Good-bye Jeff," said Aidan. "Please put The Wiggles on, Mommy. You be Murray on the way home."

———

REASON #44 ZINGERS, ONE MORE TIME

✬ ✬ ✬

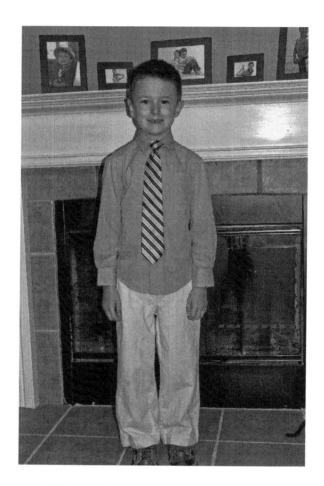

Aidan ready for a day at the theater!

- Grammie's house is located 40 yards from the railroad tracks, Aidan and I enjoyed sitting on the deck and counting the cars on the passing freight trains. After a series of 10 white tank cars had rumbled by, I commented to Aidan that they were probably carrying milk. That observation prompted this question from Aidan: "Karl, where are the brown ones for chocolate milk?"

- During a Sunday afternoon drive, Aidan pointed out that we were passing his school. "Karl, how did you know where to pick me up on our first Friday?" "Your Mommy gave me directions," I replied. "But how did Mommy know where the school was?" I reminded him of the orientation they attended before kindergarten start. Aidan put his hand to his forehead and shaking his head replied, "Oh, right. Why didn't I think of that, Karl?"

- One day I was delighted to hear this message on my answering machine. "Karl, can you come over and see our new swing set? It's awesome. Oh, this is Aidan. I love you."

- Aidan and his brother Evan had spent the day at the sitter. Mommy noticed a human bite on Aidan's arm and sought to identify the biter. Aidan had an immediate response. "Mommy, Evan did it." Evan responded just as quickly. "No, no! Mommy, I did not!" Mommy addressed Aidan directly, "Evan doesn't bite anymore, Aidan. So where did that come from?" Another heated exchange between the brothers ensued. "OK, you guys, Mommy is not angry. No one will be punished, but I need to know. Aidan, did you bite yourself?" Aidan's shoulders and head drooped. "Yes, Mommy, I did. I wanted to tell the truth," said Aidan. "But I just forgot how it happened."

- Aidan's kindergarten class took a field trip to see "The Beauty and the Beast." Aidan's fears were on the line - a bus ride, a dark theatre, and the play's characters. He called that evening. "I saw "Beauty and the Beast" today, Karl, and I'm okay. My friend Jayson sat with me on the bus and my teacher asked me to sit with her so we wouldn't be scared in the dark. Oh, and the beast? No. He wasn't scary. Just a man wearing a mask."

- I picked up Aidan at 11:30 a.m. on Friday from school as usual. On our way to lunch at McDonald's, he asked "Can we play at Jayson's house after lunch?" I explained that after lunch I really needed to go to Grammie's house and lie on the floor to rest my injured back. "Karl, that's not a problem. Jayson's house has floors."

REASON #45 Wii GAME AND KARL

✿ ✿ ✿

My VCR always blinks "12:00," my VHS movies are neatly shelved, I sometimes use my old manual Underwood typewriter, and I read four newspapers a day.

OK. So I've struggled to move into the 21st century.

Along comes Aidan and suddenly I'm supposed to understand a DS and a Wii!

Aidan's request came shortly after this new piece of technology was delivered. "Karl, you have to come over to my house and play our new Wii game. I'll teach you how. It's really neat and easy to play."

Upon arriving I was hooked up to a hand-held device and given simple instructions on how to play Tiger Woods Golf. I realized immediately that my 18-handicap on the real course would never be matched on Wii golf.

Aidan had great patience as I found water hazards and sand traps, and 8-foot putts rolled 20 feet past the hole. After every shot, Aidan stopped me to explain what I was doing wrong. "You'll get it, Karl. You'll get it. Just keep trying."

We played 9 holes; Aidan won by 12 strokes.

I was discouraged and Aidan sensed my frustration. "Karl, let's try something else. Maybe you can do better at Lego Star Wars."

After 15 minutes of watching Karl falling off cliffs, missing jumps, getting shot by lasers, and dying multiple deaths, Aidan finally accepted the futility of my efforts.

"Karl, Mommy says that you just have to be older to play some games. Maybe when you're older you'll do better. Let's go outside and hit the ball."

———

REASON #46 IT'S NOT SCARY

☆ ☆ ☆

Halloween provides an endless number of options for interacting and having fun with your grandkids -- trick or treating, designing costumes, carving pumpkins, and a visit to a haunted house together.

To Aidan "scary things" often involved the new or the unknown, and he was frequently reluctant to participate in any activity for the first time. So it was with this particular Halloween treat that I had planned.

It was on a breezy October play day, when Aidan asked, "Karl what are we going to do special today?" I was ready with a suggestion. "How about a trip to the Halloween Corn Maze?" At four and a half, Aidan loved to complete mazes in his preschool workbooks. I showed him a colorful brochure displaying an aerial view of the Corn Maze. "That'll be easy," he said confidently.

Arriving at the farm, we studied a large wall map of the eight acre Corn Maze and noted the instructions for finding ten clues located in mailboxes within the Maze. "I'm really good at finding clues," Aidan assured me.

Approaching the Corn Maze entrance I had a flashback to my days growing up in the Midwest. This tall corn was rather imposing, reaching heights of eight to ten feet or more.

Aidan became apprehensive as we stood at the entrance reading the first clue. Perhaps it was the towering stalks, or the rustling sound they made in the strong fall wind. "Karl, what if we go in and can't find our way out?" he asked. "If we get lost, Mommy will *never* find us."

I assured him that we'd be fine. "Don't worry. There are other people in the Corn Maze. We'll all find the clues, and we will not get lost." Peering into the rather dark entrance, Aidan shook his head and said "Karl, I'm scared. I don't want to go." I insisted we were going in. Aidan finally relented. "OK, I'll go, but only if you carry me."

With Aidan on my back we traversed through a decidedly difficult Corn Maze. Reaching Clue #5, we joined two adults and their two children for the rest of the journey. To my relief, Aidan wanted to walk with his peers until we finally reached the end.

The Maze exit and entrance were about 30 feet apart. As we exited, two more adults and their three small children were preparing to enter. The smallest child, perhaps age three, was close to tears and clearly afraid to enter. Aidan watched for a moment and then walked over to her. "You don't have to be afraid," he reassured her. "It's not scary. And don't worry, you can't get lost."

Aidan gave me a wide, satisfied smile as the family headed into the Corn Maze.

———

REASON #47 I LOST MY TOOTH

✫ ✫ ✫

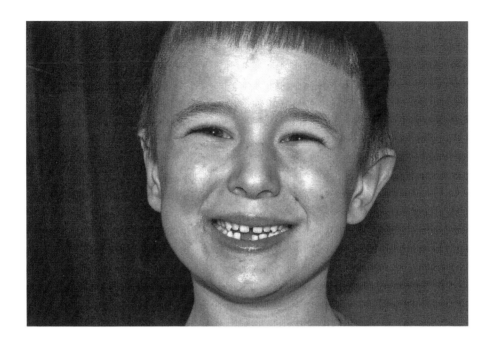

At first, nothing seemed out of the ordinary when I picked up Aidan from kindergarten at 11:30 a.m. on Friday. As usual, he jumped into my arms, waved goodbye to his teacher and his friends, and then climbed into his car seat.

He began his report. "Karl, school was awesome today. We did math and worked on our pictures of monsters. And we learned a new nursery rhyme." Suddenly he stopped talking and clapped his hand over his mouth. Tears streamed down his face. I was totally mystified and begged him to explain what was wrong. Aidan gave no reply. Just tears and "I want Mommy." I buckled him in and prepared to call Mommy. But just before I hit send, Aidan finally blurted out "Karl, it's my tooth! My tooth! Look at my tooth!"

Aidan's lower front tooth was lying flat. It was hanging on for no reason. Losing that first tooth is a traumatic life experience that most adults can remember.

I suggested that perhaps the tooth would come out with a McDonald's Happy Meal. But Aidan wanted to go directly to Grammie's house – no food and no talk.

We spent the next two hours playing quietly with Play Doh. Aidan kept his mouth closed, worked his tooth with his tongue, and periodically mumbled a few words. He did not want to open his mouth. I offered Jell-O and soup. He finally accepted a homemade milkshake for lunch.

When Daddy arrived for the 3:30 p.m. pickup, I summarized the events of the afternoon while Aidan showed Daddy the hanging tooth. Daddy assured him that it would not hurt when it eventually came out

The call came at 9:15 p.m. that evening as Daddy and Aidan were leaving a local college hockey game. "Karl! I lost my tooth at the hockey game. But don't worry. I'm OK. It's gone, but I'm OK. I'll show you the hole tomorrow."

A discussion about a visit from the Tooth Fairy had taken place earlier. Despite the late hour when Aidan and Daddy arrived at home, Aidan had plans. "Mommy, we have to send an e-mail to the Tooth Fairy *right away*." Mommy granted permission and typed while Aidan dictated:

DEAR TOOTH FAIRY: HI. MY NAME IS AIDAN. I LOST A TOOTH. I WENT TO THE HOCKEY GAME. IT WAS JUST ABOUT TO END. WHEN IT WAS THE THIRD PERIOD I LOST MY TOOTH. I WAS WATCHING THE HOCKEY GAME SO THEN I PUT MY TONGUE IN THE HOLE OF WHERE I LOST MY TOOTH. AND THEN I SAID TO DADDY, 'I LOST MY TOOTH!' I FINALLY LOST MY TOOTH. I THINK I SWALLOWED IT. THAT IS WHY I CAN'T PUT MY TOOTH UNDER THE PILLOW. THANK YOU. AIDAN

Aidan called at 9:00 a.m. the next morning. "Karl, guess what? The tooth fairy got my email and guess what? She left $10 under my pillow."

———

REASON #48 I'M ALMOST SIX NOW

✿ ✿ ✿

Birthdays. Loved by kids, dreaded by middle aged, and generally appreciated by the elderly (who understand the alternative).

Each of Aidan's birthday parties has a theme. All party accessories followed the selected theme – napkins, cups and plates, gift packages for the guests, decorations throughout the house or party location, and the large cake was decorated with words and figures to match the theme. Aidan usually wore a tee shirt signifying the theme. Mommy selected the theme for age one; thereafter it was Aidan's choice:

- First birthday: Sesame Street
- Second birthday: Shrek 2
- Third birthday: The Wiggles
- Fourth birthday: Diego
- Fifth birthday: Madagascar 2
- Sixth birthday: Star Wars

After participating in the excitement and fun of those birthday parties, grandparents not only appreciate the experience, but also are left wondering how the next one can be even more enjoyable.

Aidan loved to recite the ages of others – Mommy, Daddy, brother Evan, Grammie, Karl, and his kindergarten friends. For months before his March birthday, Aidan would mention on an almost daily basis "I am going to be six." And hold up six fingers.

As the big day approached, a Saturday afternoon party at a local bowling alley and fun center was planned. Aidan explained the arrangements to me in detail. "We're going to have my birthday party on March 19. That's not really my birthday, and, I'll still be five. But that's OK. That's the day of the party with my school friends. See, I won't be six until March 24 but it is OK to have a party when I'm still five .And when I'm really six, well, we are going to have another party at my house. And you're invited to both parties, Karl."

Arriving at his party, I watched Aidan and 11 of his boy school friends and cousins excitedly participating in candlepin bowling. Scores were not important. High fives were exchanged on most rolls.

Aidan sighted me and ran over to identify each friend. "Karl, there's Bryce and Alex and Jayson – remember, they all played T-ball with me. And that's my cousin Colin. You know him."

I shared his excitement but played grandpa and knelt down to talk quietly among the confusion. "Aidan, you have to remember to thank each of your friends for their present and … " But Aidan interrupted.

"I know, Karl and to thank them for coming. Mommy already told me. But you and Mommy didn't have to tell me. Remember, I'm almost six now."

―――

REASON #49 THERE IS NO END ...

✦ ✦ ✦

Aidan Michael

Aidan is now six years old. His days contain all the emotions of other six-year-olds – laughter, tears, joy, disappointments, excitement, worries, and more. Grandparents who spend time with their grandkids observe and feel those emotions.

There are first-time activities. Grandparents who are there experience the excitement of looking at the world with fresh eyes.

There are childhood fears and concerns. Grandparents take satisfaction in helping allay those fears and concerns.

There are learning experiences. Grandparents share in the pride of their grandkid demonstrating his or her newly learned accomplishment.

There are conversations in which precious comments, questions, and observations are expressed. Grandparents find that they love to share those conversations with others.

There is the excitement of youth. Grandparents often find themselves smiling as they recall similar experiences from their youth.

There are times when you want to trade places with your grandkids to help him or her "survive" a difficult experience (and you remember it is all part of growing up).

And there is so much more richness. There are opportunities to be the person who picks up the grandkids. The person who listens. The person who holds and comforts.

All of these opportunities have been a part of my special relationship with Aidan throughout the past six years. I'm sure those delightful experiences will be duplicated in many different ways during the next six years and beyond ... there really is no end.

✵ ✵ ✵

YOUR STORIES

All grandparents (and parents) have stories about their grandkids. Sharing those is part of the reward of spending time with your grandkids. Readers are invited to email their stories to grammierules@gmail.com. Your story could be selected for the Second Edition of "Reasons To Spend Time With Your Grandkids."

6065964R0

Made in the USA
Charleston, SC
09 September 2010